50 Perfect Pasta Dishes

STEP-BY-STEP

50 Perfect Pasta Dishes

Maxine Clark

Photography by Edward Allwright

SMITHMARK

© Anness Publishing Limited 1994

All rights reserved. No part of this publication may be
reproduced, stored in a retrieval system, or transmitted in
any way or by any means, electronic, mechanical,
photocopying, recording or otherwise, without the prior
permission of the copyright holder.

This edition published in 1994 by
SMITHMARK Publishers Inc.
16 East 32nd Street
New York
NY 10016

SMITHMARK books are available for bulk purchase for sales
promotion and for premium use. For details write or call
the manager of special sales, SMITHMARK Publishers Inc.
16 East 32nd Street, New York, 10016; (212) 532–6600

ISBN 0 8317 6515 1

Produced by Anness Publishing Limited
1 Boundary Row
London SE1 8HP

Editorial Director: Joanna Lorenz
Series Editor: Lindsay Porter
Assistant Editor: Charles Moxham
Designers: Peter Butler, Peter Laws
Home Economist: Jenny Shapter
Photographer: Edward Allwright
Stylist: Hilary Guy

Printed and bound in Italy by Graphicom S.r.l., Vicenza

CONTENTS

Introduction	**6**
PASTA SOUPS	**22**
VEGETARIAN SAUCES	**30**
MEAT AND FISH SAUCES	**48**
CLASSIC PASTA DISHES	**62**
PASTA SALADS	**78**
SWEET PASTA DISHES	**86**
Index	**96**

INTRODUCTION

Pasta has rapidly become one of today's staple foods, traveling across the world in various forms as far as Asia and South America. Its origins are unclear, but a type of pasta was certainly made in Sicily, the 'grain store' of Rome, in the days of the Roman Empire. It has also existed in China and Japan for many centuries, but in very different shapes and forms.

The enormous popularity of pasta is due to its incredible versatility, and its value for money. Pasta can stretch a few pantry ingredients to make a satisfying meal fit for a king! You can produce sauces with small amounts of meat, mix them with pasta, and produce a filling and nutritious dish. Most flour-and-water (commercial dried) pasta contains more proteins and carbohydrates than potatoes, so when combined with a sauce of vegetables, cheese, or meat, it gives a good nutritional balance. It is a fine source of energy too – better than sugar, as it releases energy at a slower, more prolonged rate, and will give you a lift if you are tired and hungry. Pasta is only fattening if eaten in over-large quantities with too much sauce! Italians fill up on the pasta itself, the sauce being an adornment to enhance the flavor.

Pasta is very easy to make at home if you have patience and a little time to spare. The result is so exciting and delicious, even if it is a little soggy to begin with! It's a little like making bread: once you have mastered the technique, you can make one of life's staples. Fresh egg pasta is made *only* with flour, eggs, a little salt, and olive oil. Do not be tempted to add water as it will toughen the pasta and make it sticky. The main thing is to enjoy the pasta-making process and the results *con gusto*.

Pasta Types

When buying dried pasta, choose good-quality well-known brands. Of the 'fresh' pasta sold in sealed packs in supermarkets, the filled or stuffed varieties are worth buying; noodles and ribbon pasta are better bought dried, as these tend to have more bite when cooked. However, if you are lucky enough to live near an Italian grocer, where pasta is made on the premises, it will usually be of very good quality. Fresh is not necessarily better, but the final choice is yours – the best pasta is homemade, as you can then be sure of the quality of the ingredients used and also of the finished texture.

You will see from this book that the sauces are almost limitless in their variety, as are the pasta shapes themselves. There are no hard-and-fast rules regarding which shape to use with which pasta sauce: it's really a matter of personal preference. However, there are a few guidelines to follow, such as that thin spaghetti suits seafood sauces, thicker spaghetti is good with creamy sauces (as in, for instance, Spaghetti alla Carbonara) and thick tubular pasta, like rigatoni, penne and so on, suits rustic sauces full of bits that will be caught in the pasta itself.

macaroni

vermicelli

quick-cook macaroni

fresh squid-ink tagliatelle

orzo or puntalette

small soup pasta

fettuccine: tomato, spinach, and plain

fresh caramellone

fettuccia riccia

fresh ravioli

fresh cappelletti

lasagne lunghe

fresh tortelloni

'paglia e fieno' ('straw and hay' tagliarini)

garganelle

spaghetti

spinach spaghetti

fresh pappardelle

*fresh beet
tagliatelle*

*fresh wild-mushroom
tagliatelle*

whole-wheat spaghetti

pipe rigate

*conchigliette rigate
(small pasta shells)*

*Pasta bows
(farfalle)*

campanelle

cannelloni

rigatoni

*pasta shells
(conchiglie)*

spirali

lasagne

spinach lasagne

whole-wheat shells

orecchiette

Herbs and Spices

Both fresh and dried herbs can be used successfully to enhance the flavor of most pasta sauces. Certain herbs have an affinity with particular ingredients, and are added to bring out their flavors or to accentuate them. Tomatoes are the natural sauce ingredient, and their taste can be changed completely by the incorporation of different herbs and spices. Fresh herbs, although expensive in supermarkets, are a must for a sauce like pesto. Dried basil has none of the Mediterranean pungency needed in this wonderfully evocative sauce. The color of fresh herbs brings a visual charm to sauces, as well as adding a truly fresh flavor. Buy growing herbs in pots and – despite instructions to the contrary on the packaging – try planting them out in the garden in summer or, as I do, in a window box. They will grow in a sunny, well-drained spot if cut regularly (but not too much). Stating that they cannot be planted out is a commercial ploy to make you buy more.

Ideally use fresh herbs immediately after cutting, but if you have to keep them for any length of time, most will store well in a jar of water covered with a sealed plastic bag and placed in the refrigerator.

Dried herbs are very useful if they are not too old. Freeze-dried are the best as they retain both color and flavor. Use half the quantity of dried herbs as you would fresh, for the flavor is more concentrated. Always store dried herbs in airtight containers, in a dark, dry cupboard.

Arugula
Arugula, with its slightly peppery taste, can be used both as an herb and, more commonly, as a salad ingredient. In this book it is simply stirred into a pasta dish at the end of cooking so that it wilts like spinach, but is still crunchy.

Basil
Fresh basil is *the* herb for pasta dishes, and dried basil is a poor substitute. If fresh basil is unavailable, use a spoonful of ready-made pesto sauce instead of the dried herb for a better taste. The flavor is a pungent mixture of cinnamon and anise: it is too difficult to describe, so just find some and use it – the more, the better! Basil is wonderful with tomatoes and in delicate ricotta cheese fillings. It is lost, however, in hearty meaty sauces.

Bay leaves
Bay is often used to enhance the flavor of meat sauces and to give a delicate flavor to béchamel or white sauces.

Dill
An herb with a slightly aniseed flavor that marries well with fish, especially fresh or smoked salmon.

Garlic
Used in moderation, garlic is a marvelous flavor enhancer. However, the longer you cook it, the more mellow the flavor. It is good in most dishes where a strong onion taste is required – meat sauces, anything with tomato, and with legumes and beans. Choose big fat cloves for a fuller, less bitter flavor.

Oregano and marjoram
Oregano and marjoram are the most popular herbs used in Italy, along with basil and sage. They have an affinity with tomatoes and eggs, and make a pretty garnish when in flower. Oregano is a wilder strain and more astringent than marjoram, which has a sweeter flavor.

Parsley (curly and flat-leaf)
Parsley is a very versatile herb and both types of parsley impart a fresh 'green' flavor to almost any dish. The common curly variety is good for chopping and the pretty flat-leafed one can be roughly chopped or used as a leafy garnish. A delicious pesto sauce can be made using parsley instead of basil.

Sage
A classic Italian herb available in many varieties. It has a lovely earthy flavor and is good with meat and some cheeses such as Gorgonzola.

Chilies (dried and fresh)
Use smaller quantities of dried chilies than fresh – they add heat and spiciness to sauces such as arrabbiata. Wear rubber gloves when preparing fresh chilies, or work under running water, and don't rub your eyes as the juice of both dried and fresh chilies can be painful. Green or red chilies can be used – the quantities are variable depending on your taste, but to be on the safe side, add less than specified in the recipe: you can always add more.

Nutmeg
The kernel of a nut that also produces mace, nutmeg gives a rich musky flavor to white sauces and is good with cheese.

Saffron
These orange filaments are the stigmas of the saffron crocus, one of the world's most expensive spices, but a little goes a long way. Saffron is also available in powdered form. This delicate spice will impart a wonderful aroma and color to any dish.

dried chilies

bay

saffron

arugula

oregano

dill

sage

fresh chilies

garlic

basil

flat-leaf parsley

curly parsley

nutmeg

purple marjoram

Sauces and Pastes

There is an infinite variety of ready-made sauces and pastes available that you can add to your own sauce to make it richer or to deepen the flavor. Some can even be incorporated into pasta dough: for example, you can make mushroom or tomato or even pesto pasta.

Anchovies: salted
Whole anchovies preserved in salt need to be rinsed and the backbone should be removed before use. They have a a fresher flavor than canned anchovies in oil. Used in moderation, anchovies add a fishy depth to sauces and soups.

Capers
These are little green flower buds picked before they open and preserved in vinegar or salt. They add a sharp piquancy to rich sauces and are particularly good with tomatoes and cheese.

Carbonara sauce
Although your own version made from the recipe in this book will be much better, ready-made carbonara sauce is a useful standby for a quick meal – add sautéed fresh mushrooms or more bacon to make it go further.

Garlic: chopped
A great time-saver, eliminating the need for peeling and chopping. Use it straight out of the jar.

Mushroom paste
A delicacy available from Italian grocers. Add a generous spoonful to freshly cooked pasta with a little cream for a quick sauce, or to pasta dough to make mushroom pasta.

Olive paste
Cuts out all that pitting and chopping. Delicious stirred into hot pasta with chopped fresh tomato or added by the spoonful to enrich a tomato or meat sauce.

Pesto
The commercial version of fresh basil pesto. Brands vary, but it is a very useful pantry standby to stir into hot pasta and soups.

Pesto: fresh
Some supermarkets produce their own 'fresh' pesto, sold in tubs in the refrigerated section. This is superior to the bottled variety, although your own freshly made pesto will be even better.

Pesto: red
A commercial sauce made from tomatoes and sun-dried tomatoes to stir into hot pasta or soups.

Tomato pasta sauce
Again, a good standby or base for a quick meal. Vary by adding chopped anchovies and olives, or add to sautéed ground meat to make a quick and easy Bolognese sauce or pour over freshly cooked stuffed pasta.

Tomato paste
An essential if you are making a sauce from insipid fresh tomatoes! It will intensify the color and flavor of any tomato-based sauce and will help thicken meat sauces. It will also make tomato pasta if added to the basic ingredients.

Tomatoes: canned plum
No pantry should be without these – invaluable for making any tomato sauce or stew at a minute's notice or when good fresh tomatoes are not available.

Tomatoes: canned chopped
Usually made from Italian plum tomatoes, that have a fuller flavor than most, these are the heart of a good tomato sauce if you cannot find really ripe red tasty fresh tomatoes.

Tomatoes: coulis (strained crushed tomatoes)
A useful pantry ingredient, this is tomato that has been strained to remove the seeds. It makes a good base for a smooth tomato sauce, though chopped canned tomatoes can also be used.

Tomatoes: sun-dried in oil
These tomatoes are drained and chopped and added to tomato-based dishes to give a deeper, almost roasted tomato flavor.

Left: *There are many ready-prepared sauces and pastes available. From top left: tomato coulis, salted anchovies, mushroom paste, olive paste, tomato paste, chopped tomato, carbonara sauce, canned plum tomatoes, capers, tomato pasta sauce, red pesto, pesto, fresh pesto, sun-dried tomatoes in oil, chopped garlic.*

Eastern Pasta

Various forms of noodle or pasta exist outside Europe. They are found mainly in China and Japan, but also throughout Malaysia, Hong Kong, and the rest of the Far East, including parts of India and Tibet.

This pasta, usually in noodle form and often enhanced with a sprinkling of vegetables or fish, adds variety to the sometimes monotonous staple diet of rice and beans eaten by the poorer sections of the population. Some types of pasta are used to give bulk to soups; others are eaten as a filling dish to stave off hunger during the day. They are made from the staple crops of each region – whether rice flour, soy bean flour or potato flour – and are cooked in different ways: some are soaked and then fried, some are boiled and fried and some are rolled out and stuffed like ravioli, but most are simply boiled. Some turn transparent when cooked.

Oriental egg noodles are usually made with wheat flour and can be treated in the same way as ordinary Western pasta. Buckwheat and fresh whole-wheat noodles are similarly cooked. Fresh white noodles do not contain egg but are cooked in the same way as egg noodles. Some dried egg noodles come in disks or blocks and are 'cooked' by immersion in boiling water in which they are then left to soak for a few minutes. As with Western pasta, oriental noodles can be flavored with other ingredients such as shrimp, carrot, and spinach. Wonton skins, like thin squares of rolled-out pasta, are used for stuffing and making different filled shapes. Although

oriental pasta is available in a variety of long noodle types, it doesn't seem to be made into the variety of shapes and sizes we are used to seeing in Europe and America: you will often find it wound into balls and presented in beautiful packaging.

Above: *Eastern noodles include (from top left, clockwise) Oriental rice flour noodles, rice vermicelli, rice stick noodles, hand-made amoy flour vermicelli, medium egg noodles, fresh brown mein, egg noodles, rice stick vermicelli, fresh thin egg noodles, Japanese wheat flour noodles, Ho Fan vermicelli, spinach vegetable noodles, carrot vegetable noodles, won ton skins, wheat flour noodles, fresh white mein, buckwheat noodles, shrimp egg noodles.*

Basic Sauce Ingredients

Bell Peppers: red and yellow
Red and yellow peppers make a delicious addition to a sauce and are good with cold pasta salad.

Clams
Small clams are best for sauces and soups. Fresh mussels are a good substitute, as are canned clams in brine.

Dolcelatte
An Italian, blue-veined, creamy cheese used in sauces and fillings.

Feta
Feta is firm and crumbly with a salty taste from the brine in which it is preserved.

Gorgonzola
An Italian, blue-veined, semi-soft cheese with a piquant flavor. Used in sauces and stuffings.

Italian sausages
Meaty, highly seasoned fresh sausages used to make quick sauces and stuffings.

Mediterranean shrimp
Raw or cooked, these large shrimp have more flavor than smaller varieties. Gulf shrimp are a good substitute.

Mussels
As with clams, mussels are best fresh, but frozen cooked ones can be substituted.

Olives
Used in sauces to add richness, black olives have more flavor than the green kind.

Onions
Spanish onions add sweetness and red or purple types add a mild flavor and attractive color.

Pancetta
Italian bacon sold smoked or unsmoked, sliced or in a piece, to add flavor to sauces.

Parmesan
A hard cheese for grating and serving with pasta, made from semi-skimmed unpasteurized cow's milk.

Pine nuts
These small creamy-colored nuts are essential in pesto.

Pistachios
Pale green nuts from the Middle East that are used in sweet and savory dishes.

Ricotta
An Italian whey cheese that is soft and creamy. It is especially good in sweet or savory fillings.

Smoked salmon
Cold smoked salmon can be thinly sliced and added to sauces and fillings.

Spinach
Spinach is an iron-rich, leafy, green vegetable mainly used to flavor and color pasta dough.

Tomatoes
Choose only really ripe tomatoes – plum if possible. Miniature or cherry tomatoes make a good addition to sauces.

Walnuts
Walnuts are used in sweet and savory dishes. They are also used in walnut pesto.

black olives

smoked salmon

pancetta

spinach

Italian sausages

feta

Parmesan

red and yellow bell peppers

Gorgonzola

onions

Dolcelatte

mussels

pistachios

ricotta

clams

pine nuts

pear tomatoes

plum tomato

walnuts

Mediterranean
shrimp

cherry tomatoes

Equipment

To make pasta, a bare minimum of equipment is needed – practiced hands would say that only a clean table top and a rolling pin were necessary. However, there are several gadgets to make pasta making easier.

Bowls
A set of bowls is useful for mixing, whisking and so on.

Chopping board
A hygienic nylon board is recommended for cutting and chopping.

Colander
A large colander is essential for draining cooked pasta quickly.

Cook's knife
A large all-purpose cook's knife is essential for cutting pasta and for chopping.

Flour dredger
Useful for dusting pasta with small amounts of flour.

Large metal spoon
For folding in and serving sauces.

Measuring spoons
For accurately measuring quantities of ingredients.

Pasta machine or roller
Vital for kneading, rolling, and cutting pasta – a real labor-saver. Attachments for other shapes are available.

Pasta or pastry wheel
For cutting shapes, such as pasta bows, with a decorated edge.

Pastry brush
For removing excess flour from pasta and for brushing pasta with water, milk, or beaten egg to seal.

Perforated spoon
Useful for draining small amounts of food.

Pestle and mortar
For hand-grinding pesto and crushing black peppercorns.

Ravioli cutter
For cutting or stamping out individual raviolis; can be round or square. A selection of pastry cutters will serve the same purpose.

Ravioli tray (raviolatore)
For making sheets of ravioli quickly and neatly – with practice!

Rolling pin
Pasta pins are available in some kitchenware stores. These are long, thin, and tapered at each end, but you have to be quite adept to use them. An ordinary heavy wooden rolling pin will do.

Small grater
For freshly grating nutmeg and Parmesan cheese.

Vegetable knife
For preparing vegetables and paring lemons, and for delicate work.

Vegetable peeler
For shaving Parmesan cheese and chocolate.

Whisk
An essential item for beating eggs thoroughly and combining sauces smoothly.

bowls

pasta machine

cook's knife

measuring spoons

flour dredger

rolling pin

pestle and mortar

cutters

colander

perforated spoon

large metal spoon

chopping board

vegetable knife

pastry brush

metal whisk

vegetable peeler

pastry wheel

small grater

ravioli cutter

ravioli tray

To Cook Pasta

1 Throw the pasta into a large pan of boiling salted water. Stir once to prevent sticking. The addition of 1 tbsp vegetable or olive oil will help to stop the water boiling over and prevent the pasta from sticking. *Do not cover* the pan or the water will boil over.

2 Quickly bring the pasta back to a rolling boil and boil until *al dente* (literally 'to the tooth') – the pasta should be just firm to the bite. It should not have a hard center or be very floppy.

3 Quickly drain the pasta well, using a large colander or strainer. Immediately rinse the pasta with boiling water to wash off any starch and to prevent the pasta from sticking together. At this stage you can toss the pasta in a little olive oil or butter if not dressing with the sauce immediately. Serve hot pasta straight away. It is up to you whether you toss the pasta with the sauce before serving or serve it with the sauce on top.

COOKING TIMES FOR FRESH AND DRIED PASTA

Calculate the cooking time from the moment the water returns to a boil after the pasta has been added.

Unfilled pasta
Fresh: 2–3 minutes, though some very thin pasta is ready as soon as the water returns to the boil.
Dried: 8–12 minutes, but keep checking as this is only a guide.

Filled pasta
Fresh: 8–10 minutes.
Dried: 15–20 minutes.

Basic Pasta Dough

Allow 1¾ cups all-purpose flour, a pinch of salt, and 1 tbsp olive oil to 2 eggs for 3–4 servings, depending on the required size of portion.

1 Sift the flour and salt onto a clean work surface and make a well in the center with your fist.

2 Pour the beaten eggs and oil into the well. Gradually mix the eggs into the flour with the fingers of one hand.

3 Knead the pasta until smooth, wrap, and allow to rest for at least 30 minutes before attempting to roll out. The pasta will be much more elastic after resting.

Using a Food Processor

1 Sift the flour into the bowl and add a pinch of salt.

2 Pour in the beaten eggs and oil and any chosen flavoring, and process until the dough begins to come together.

3 Tip out the dough and knead until smooth. Wrap and rest for 30 minutes. Use as required.

Using a Pasta Machine

1 Feed the rested dough several times through the highest setting first, then reducing the settings until the required thickness is achieved.

2 A special cutter will produce fettuccine or tagliatelle.

3 A narrower cutter will produce spaghetti or tagliarini.

COOK'S TIP
These are only guidelines: depending on the air humidity, the type of flour and so on, you may have to add more flour. The dough must not be too soft – it should be quite hard to knead. Too much extra flour will make the pasta tough and taste floury!

WATER NEEDED TO COOK PASTA
4½ quarts water plus 3 tbsp salt for every 11 oz–1 lb dried pasta or 11 oz–1 lb fresh pasta. This will prevent the pasta from sticking.

FLAVORED PASTA
Tomato Pasta
Add 2 tbsp tomato paste to the flour. Use about 1½ eggs.

Beet Pasta
Add 2 tbsp grated cooked beet to the flour. Use about 1½ eggs.

Saffron Pasta
Soak a packet of powdered saffron in 2 tbsp hot water for 15 minutes. Use 1½ eggs and whisk the saffron water into them.

Herb Pasta
Add 3 tbsp chopped fresh herbs to the flour.

Whole-wheat Pasta
Use 1¼ cups whole-wheat flour sifted with ¼ cup all-purpose flour and 2 eggs.

Macaroni

Macaroni is the generic name for any hollow pasta. This method is for making garganelle.

1 Cut squares of pasta dough using a sharp knife on a floured surface.

2 Wrap the squares around a pencil or chopstick on the diagonal to form tubes. Slip off and allow to dry slightly.

SPINACH PASTA

Use 5 oz frozen leaf spinach, cooked and squeezed of as much moisture as possible, a pinch of salt, 2 eggs, and about 1¾ cups all-purpose flour (the pasta may need a little more if sticky). Proceed as in the recipe for Basic Pasta Dough, but liquidize the spinach with the eggs to give a fine texture to the dough.

Tagliatelle

Tagliatelle can also be made with a pasta machine, but it is fairly straightforward to make it by hand.

1 Roll up the floured pasta dough like a jelly roll.

2 Cut the roll into thin slices with a sharp knife. Immediately unravel the slices to reveal the pasta ribbons. To make tagliarini cut the slices ⅛ in thick.

3 To make pappardelle, using a serrated pastry wheel, cut out wide ribbons from the rolled pasta dough.

Tortellini

Tortellini or 'little twists' can be made with meat or vegetarian fillings and served with sauce or in a soup.

1 Using a round cookie cutter, stamp out rounds of pasta.

2 Pipe or spoon the chosen filling into the middle of each round.

3 Brush the edges with beaten egg and fold the round into a crescent shape, excluding all the air. Bend the 2 corners round to meet each other and press well to seal. Repeat with the remaining dough. Leave to dry on a floured dish towel for 30 minutes before cooking.

SPINACH, RICOTTA, AND PARMESAN FILLING FOR STUFFED PASTA
Serves 4–6

1 lb frozen spinach, thawed and
   squeezed dry
½ tsp freshly grated nutmeg
1 tsp salt
freshly ground black pepper
¾ cup fresh ricotta or cottage cheese
¼ cup freshly grated Parmesan
   cheese

Place all the ingredients in a food processor and process until smooth. Use as required.

Ravioli

Although ravioli can be bought ready made, the very best is made at home. Serve with sauce or in a soup.

1 Cut the dough in half and wrap one portion in plastic wrap. Roll out the pasta thinly to a rectangle on a lightly floured surface. Cover with a clean damp dish towel and repeat with the remaining pasta. Pipe small mounds (about 1 tsp) of filling in even rows, spacing them at 1 ½ in intervals, across one piece of the dough. Brush the spaces between the filling with beaten egg.

2 Using a rolling pin, lift the remaining sheet of pasta over the dough with the filling. Press down firmly between the pockets of filling, pushing out any air.

3 Cut into squares with a serrated ravioli cutter or sharp knife. Transfer to a floured dish towel and rest for 1 hour before cooking.

Minestrone

A classic substantial winter soup originally from Milan, but found in various versions around the Mediterranean coasts of Italy and France. Cut the vegetables as roughly or as small as you like. Add freshly grated Parmesan cheese just before serving.

Serves 6–8

INGREDIENTS
2 cups dried white beans
2 tbsp olive oil
2 oz bacon, diced
2 large onions, sliced
2 garlic cloves, crushed
2 medium carrots, diced
3 celery sticks, sliced
14 oz canned chopped tomatoes
10 cups beef stock
12 oz potatoes, diced
1½ cups small pasta shapes
   (macaroni, stars, shells, etc)
½ lb green cabbage, thinly sliced
6 oz fine green beans, sliced
¾ cup frozen peas
3 tbsp chopped fresh parsley
salt and pepper
freshly grated Parmesan cheese,
   to serve

1 Cover the beans with cold water and leave to soak overnight.

2 Heat the oil in a large saucepan and add the bacon, onions, and garlic. Cover and cook gently for 5 minutes, stirring occasionally, until soft.

3 Add the carrots and celery and cook for 2–3 minutes until softening.

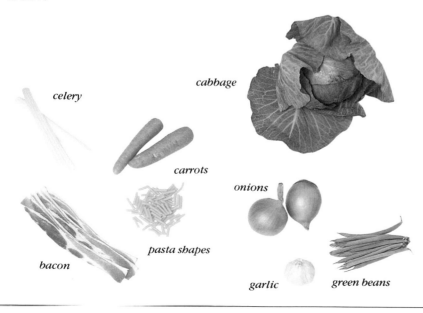

celery

cabbage

carrots

onions

pasta shapes

bacon

garlic   *green beans*

4 Drain the beans and add to the pan with the tomatoes and stock. Cover and simmer for 2–2½ hours, until the beans are tender.

5 Add the potatoes 30 minutes before the soup is finished.

VARIATION

To make Soupe au Pistou from the South of France, stir in a basil, garlic and pine nut sauce (pesto or pistou) just before serving.

6 Add the pasta, cabbage, beans, peas, and parsley 15 minutes before the soup is ready. Season to taste and serve with a bowl of freshly grated Parmesan cheese.

Italian Bean and Pasta Soup

A thick and hearty soup which, followed by bread and
cheese, makes a substantial lunch.

Serves 6

INGREDIENTS
1½ cups dried white beans, soaked
   overnight in cold water
7½ cups chicken stock or water
1 cup medium pasta shells
4 tbsp olive oil, plus extra to serve
2 garlic cloves, crushed
4 tbsp chopped fresh parsley
salt and pepper

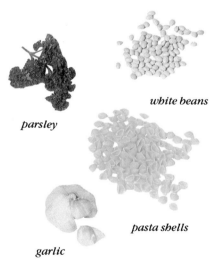

parsley

white beans

pasta shells

garlic

1 Drain the beans and place in a large
saucepan with the stock or water.
Simmer, half-covered, for 2–2½ hours or
until tender.

2 Liquidize half the beans and a little of
their cooking liquid, then stir into the
remaining beans in the pan.

3 Add the pasta and simmer gently for
15 minutes until tender. (Add extra water
or stock if the soup seems too thick.)

4 Heat the oil in a small pan and fry the
garlic until golden. Stir into the soup with
the parsley and season well with salt and
pepper. Ladle into individual bowls and
drizzle each with a little extra olive oil.

Zucchini Soup with Small Pasta Shells

A pretty, fresh-tasting soup which could be made using cucumber instead of zucchini.

Serves 4–6

INGREDIENTS
4 tbsp olive or sunflower oil
2 medium onions, finely chopped
6¼ cups chicken stock
2 lb zucchini
1 cup small soup pasta
fresh lemon juice
salt and pepper
2 tbsp chopped fresh chervil
sour cream, to serve

zucchini

onion

soup pasta

chervil

1 Heat the oil in a large saucepan and add the onions. Cover and cook gently for about 20 minutes until very soft but not colored, stirring occasionally.

2 Add the stock and bring to the boil.

3 Meanwhile grate the zucchini and stir into the boiling stock with the pasta. Turn down the heat and simmer for 15 minutes until the pasta is tender. Season to taste with lemon juice, salt, and pepper.

4 Stir in the chervil and add a swirl of sour cream before serving.

COOK'S TIP
If no fresh stock is available, instead of using a stock cube, use canned chicken or beef consommé.

Provençal Fish Soup with Pasta

This colorful soup has all the flavors of the Mediterranean. Serve it as a main course for a deliciously filling lunch.

Serves 4

INGREDIENTS
2 tbsp olive oil
1 medium onion, sliced
1 garlic clove, crushed
1 leek, sliced
8 oz canned chopped tomatoes
pinch of herbes de Provence
¼ tsp saffron threads (optional)
1 cup small pasta
salt and pepper
about 8 live mussels
1 lb filleted and skinned white fish
    (cod, plaice, monkfish)

ROUILLE
2 garlic cloves, crushed
1 canned pimento, drained and
    chopped
1 tbsp fresh white bread crumbs
4 tbsp mayonnaise
toasted French bread, to serve

pasta

white fish

garlic

onion

mussels

leek

1 Heat the oil in a large saucepan and add the onion, garlic, and leek. Cover and cook gently for 5 minutes, stirring occasionally until soft.

2 Pour in 4½ cups water, the tomatoes, herbs, saffron, and pasta. Season with salt and pepper and cook for 15–20 minutes.

3 Scrub the mussels and pull off the 'beards'. Discard any that will not close when sharply tapped: they are almost certainly dead.

4 Cut the fish into bite-sized chunks and add to the soup, placing the mussels on top. Simmer with the lid on for 5–10 minutes until the mussels open and the fish is just cooked. (If any mussels fail to open, discard them.)

5 To make the *rouille*, pound the garlic, canned pimento, and bread crumbs together in a pestle and mortar (or in a food processor). Stir in the mayonnaise and season well.

6 Spread the toasted French bread with the *rouille* and serve with the soup.

Chicken Vermicelli Soup with Egg Shreds

This soup is very quick and easy – you can add all sorts of extra ingredients to vary the taste, using up lurking leftovers such as scallions, mushrooms, a few shrimp, chopped salami and so on.

Serves 4–6

INGREDIENTS
3 large eggs
2 tbsp chopped fresh cilantro or
    parsley
6¼ cups good chicken stock or
    canned consommé
1 cup dried vermicelli or angel hair
    pasta
¼ lb cooked chicken breast, sliced
salt and pepper

vermicelli

chicken breast

eggs

cilantro

1 First make the egg shreds. Whisk the eggs together in a small bowl and stir in the cilantro or parsley.

THAI CHICKEN SOUP

To make a Thai variation, use Chinese rice noodles instead of pasta. Stir ½ tsp dried lemon grass, 2 small whole fresh chilies and 4 tbsp coconut milk into the stock. Add 4 sliced scallions and plenty of chopped fresh cilantro.

2 Heat a small nonstick skillet and pour in 2–3 tbsp egg, swirling to cover the base evenly. Cook until set. Repeat until all the mixture is used up.

3 Roll each pancake up and slice thinly into shreds. Set aside.

4 Bring the stock to a boil and add the pasta, breaking it up into short lengths. Cook for 3–5 minutes until the pasta is almost tender, then add the chicken, salt, and pepper. Heat through for 2–3 minutes, then stir in the egg shreds. Serve immediately.

Creamy Parmesan and Cauliflower Soup with Pasta Bows

A silky smooth, mildly cheesy soup that isn't overpowered by the cauliflower. It is an elegant dinner party soup served with the crisp melba toast.

Serves 6

INGREDIENTS
1 large cauliflower
5 cups chicken or vegetable stock
1½ cups pasta bows (farfalle)
⅔ cup light cream or milk
freshly grated nutmeg
pinch of cayenne pepper
4 tbsp freshly grated Parmesan cheese
salt and pepper

MELBA TOAST
3–4 slices day-old white bread
freshly grated Parmesan cheese, for
   sprinkling
¼ tsp paprika

cauliflower

pasta bows

Parmesan cheese

nutmeg

1 Cut the leaves and central stalk away from the cauliflower and discard. Divide the cauliflower into florets.

2 Bring the stock to a boil and add the cauliflower. Simmer for about 10 minutes or until very soft. Remove the cauliflower with a perforated spoon and place in a food processor.

3 Add the pasta to the stock and simmer for 10 minutes until tender. Drain, reserve the pasta, and pour the liquid over the cauliflower in the food processor. Add the cream or milk, nutmeg, and cayenne to the cauliflower. Blend until smooth, then press through a strainer. Stir in the cooked pasta. Reheat the soup and stir in the Parmesan. Taste and adjust the seasoning.

4 Meanwhile make the melba toast. Preheat the oven to 350°F. Toast the bread lightly on both sides. Quickly cut off the crusts and split each slice in half horizontally. Scrape off any doughy bits and sprinkle with Parmesan and paprika. Place on a baking sheet and bake in the oven for 10–15 minutes or until uniformly golden. Serve with the soup.

Pasta with Roasted Bell Pepper and Tomato Sauce

Add other vegetables such as French beans or zucchini or even chick peas (garbanzos) to make this sauce more substantial.

Serves 4

INGREDIENTS
2 medium red bell peppers
2 medium yellow bell peppers
3 tbsp olive oil
1 medium onion, sliced
2 garlic cloves, crushed
½ tsp mild chili powder
14 oz canned chopped plum tomatoes
salt and pepper
4 cups dried pasta shells or spirals
freshly grated Parmesan cheese, to
    serve

bell peppers

pasta shells

onion

garlic

1 Preheat the oven to 400°F. Place the bell peppers on a baking sheet or in a roasting pan and bake for about 20 minutes or until beginning to char. Alternatively broil the peppers, turning frequently.

2 Rub the skins off the peppers under cold water. Halve, remove the seeds, and roughly chop the flesh.

3 Heat the oil in a medium saucepan and add the onion and garlic. Cook gently for 5 minutes until soft and golden.

4 Stir in the chili powder, cook for 2 minutes, then add the tomatoes and peppers. Bring to a boil and simmer for 10–15 minutes until slightly thickened and reduced. Season to taste.

5 Cook the pasta in plenty of boiling salted water according to the manufacturer's instructions. Drain well and toss with the sauce. Serve piping hot with lots of Parmesan cheese.

Tagliatelle with Walnut Sauce

An unusual sauce that would make this a spectacular dinner party starter.

Serves 4–6

INGREDIENTS
2 thick slices whole-wheat bread
1¼ cups milk
2½ cups walnut pieces
1 garlic clove, crushed
½ cup freshly grated Parmesan cheese
6 tbsp olive oil, plus extra for tossing the pasta
salt and pepper
⅓ cup heavy cream (optional)
1 lb tagliatelle
2 tbsp chopped fresh parsley

1 Cut the crusts off the bread and soak in the milk until the milk is all absorbed.

2 Preheat the oven to 375°F. Spread the walnuts on a baking sheet and toast in the oven for 5 minutes. Leave to cool.

3 Place the bread, walnuts, garlic, Parmesan cheese, and olive oil in a food processor and blend until smooth. Season to taste with salt and pepper. Stir in the cream, if using.

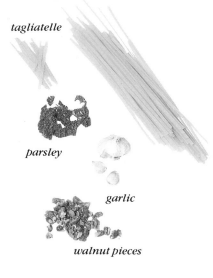

tagliatelle

parsley

garlic

walnut pieces

4 Cook the pasta in plenty of boiling salted water, drain, and toss with a little olive oil. Divide the pasta equally between 4 bowls and place a dollop of sauce on each portion. Sprinkle liberally with parsley.

VARIATION

Add ¾ cup pitted black olives to the food processor with the other ingredients for a richer, more piquant sauce. The Greek-style olives have the most flavor.

Stir-fried Vegetables with Pasta

This is a colorful Chinese-style dish, easily prepared using pasta instead of Chinese noodles.

Serves 4

INGREDIENTS
1 medium carrot
6 oz small zucchini
6 oz green beans
6 oz baby corn
1 lb ribbon pasta such as tagliatelle
salt
2 tbsp corn oil, plus extra for tossing
   the pasta
½ in piece fresh ginger, peeled and
   finely chopped
2 garlic cloves, finely chopped
6 tbsp yellow bean sauce
6 scallions, sliced into 1 in lengths
2 tbsp dry sherry
1 tsp sesame seeds

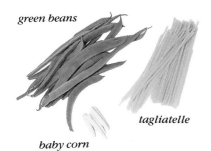

green beans

tagliatelle

baby corn

ginger

scallions

zucchini

garlic

1 Slice the carrot and zucchini diagonally into chunks. Slice the beans diagonally. Cut the baby corn diagonally in half.

2 Cook the pasta in plenty of boiling salted water according to the manufacturer's instructions, drain, then rinse under hot water. Toss in a little oil.

3 Heat 2 tbsp oil until smoking in a wok or skillet and add the ginger and garlic. Stir-fry for 30 seconds, then add the carrots, beans, and zucchini.

4 Stir-fry for 3–4 minutes, then stir in the yellow bean sauce. Stir-fry for 2 minutes, add the scallions, sherry, and pasta and stir-fry for 1 minute more until piping hot. Sprinkle with sesame seeds and serve immediately.

Spaghetti with Fresh Tomato Sauce

The heat from the pasta will release the delicious flavors of this sauce. Only use the really red and soft tomatoes – large ripe beefsteak tomatoes are ideal. Don't be tempted to use small hard tomatoes: they have very little flavor.

Serves 4

INGREDIENTS
4 large ripe tomatoes
2 garlic cloves, finely chopped
4 tbsp chopped fresh herbs such as
   basil, marjoram, oregano, or parsley
⅔ cup olive oil
salt and pepper
1 lb spaghetti

2 Lift out with a perforated spoon and plunge into a bowl of cold water. Peel off the skins, then dry the tomatoes on paper towels.

3 Halve the tomatoes and squeeze out the seeds. Chop into ¼ in cubes and mix with the garlic, herbs, olive oil, and seasoning in a non-metallic bowl. Cover and allow the flavors to mellow for at least 30 minutes.

olive oil

garlic

spaghetti

tomato

1 Skin the tomatoes by placing in boiling water for 1 minute – no longer or they will become mushy.

VARIATION
Mix ¾ cup pitted and chopped black Greek-style olives into the sauce just before serving.

4 Cook the pasta in plenty of boiling salted water.

5 Drain the pasta and mix with the sauce. Cover with a lid and leave for 2–3 minutes, toss again, and serve immediately.

Tagliatelle with Gorgonzola Sauce

Gorgonzola is a creamy Italian blue cheese. As an alternative you could use Danish Blue.

Serves 4

INGREDIENTS
2 tbsp butter, plus extra for tossing
   the pasta
½ lb Gorgonzola cheese
⅔ cup heavy or whipping cream
2 tbsp dry vermouth
1 tsp cornstarch
1 tbsp chopped fresh sage
salt and pepper
1 lb tagliatelle

tagliatelle

Gorgonzola cheese

sage

1 Melt 2 tbsp butter in a heavy saucepan (it needs to be thick-based to prevent the cheese from burning). Stir in 6 oz crumbled Gorgonzola cheese and stir over a very gentle heat for 2–3 minutes until the cheese is melted.

2 Pour in the cream, vermouth, and cornstarch, whisking well to amalgamate. Stir in the chopped sage, then taste and season. Cook, whisking all the time, until the sauce boils and thickens. Set aside.

3 Boil the pasta in plenty of salted water according to the manufacturer's instructions. Drain well and toss with a little butter.

4 Reheat the sauce gently, whisking well. Divide the pasta between 4 serving bowls, top with the sauce, and sprinkle over the remaining cheese. Serve immediately.

Pasta with Tomato and Cream Sauce

Here pasta is served with a deliciously rich version of ordinary tomato sauce.

Serves 4–6

INGREDIENTS
2 tbsp olive oil
2 garlic cloves, crushed
14 oz canned chopped tomatoes
⅔ cup heavy or whipping cream
2 tbsp chopped fresh herbs such as
    basil, oregano, or parsley
salt and pepper
4 cups pasta, any variety

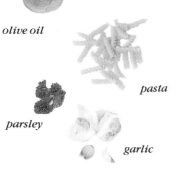

olive oil

chopped tomatoes

parsley

pasta

garlic

1 Heat the oil in a medium saucepan, add the garlic, and cook for 2 minutes until golden.

COOK'S TIP

If you are really in a hurry, buy a good ready-made tomato sauce and simply stir in the cream and simmer until thickened.

2 Stir in the tomatoes, bring to a boil and simmer uncovered for 20 minutes, stirring occasionally to prevent sticking. The sauce is ready when you can see the oil separating on top.

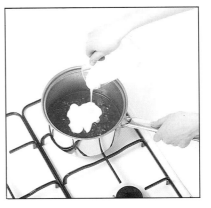

3 Add the cream, bring slowly to a boil again, and simmer until slightly thickened. Stir in the herbs, taste, and season well.

4 Cook the pasta in plenty of boiling salted water according to the manufacturer's instructions. Drain well and toss with the sauce. Serve piping hot, sprinkled with extra herbs if liked.

Rigatoni with Garlic Crumbs

A hot and spicy dish – halve the quantity of chili if you like a milder flavor. The bacon is an addition for meat-eaters; leave it out or replace it with sliced mushrooms, if you prefer.

Serves 4–6

INGREDIENTS
3 tbsp olive oil
2 shallots, chopped
8 slices bacon, chopped (optional)
2 tsp crushed dried chilies
14 oz canned chopped tomatoes with garlic and herbs
6 slices white bread
½ cup butter
2 garlic cloves, chopped
1 lb rigatoni
salt and pepper

olive oil

garlic

rigatoni

shallots　　*dried chilies*

1 Heat the oil in a medium saucepan and fry the shallots and bacon gently for 6–8 minutes until golden. Add the dried chilies and chopped tomatoes, half-cover, and simmer for 20 minutes.

2 Meanwhile cut the crusts off the bread and discard them. Reduce the bread to crumbs in a food processor.

3 Heat the butter in a skillet, add the garlic and bread crumbs and stir-fry until golden and crisp. (Don't let the crumbs catch and burn or the dish will be ruined!)

4 Cook the pasta in boiling salted water according to the manufacturer's instructions. Drain well.

5 Toss the pasta with the tomato sauce and divide between 4 serving bowls.

6 Sprinkle with the crumbs and serve immediately.

Tortellini with Cream, Butter and Cheese

This is an indulgent but quick alternative to macaroni and cheese. Meat-eaters could stir in some ham or pepperoni, though it's delicious as it is!

Serves 4–6

INGREDIENTS
4 cups fresh tortellini
salt and pepper
4 tbsp butter
1¼ cups heavy cream
¼ lb piece fresh Parmesan cheese
freshly grated nutmeg

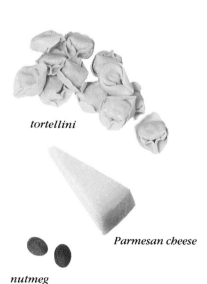

tortellini

Parmesan cheese

nutmeg

COOK'S TIP
Other hard grating cheeses can be used here, but don't try to use light cream or it will curdle.

1 Cook the pasta in plenty of boiling salted water according to the manufacturer's instructions.

2 Meanwhile melt the butter in a medium saucepan and stir in the cream. Bring to a boil and cook for 2–3 minutes until slightly thickened.

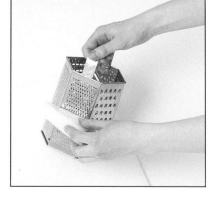

3 Grate the Parmesan cheese and stir ¾ cup into the sauce until melted. Season to taste with salt, pepper, and nutmeg. Preheat the broiler.

4 Drain the pasta well and spoon into a buttered heatproof serving dish. Pour over the sauce, sprinkle over the remaining cheese, and place under the broiler until brown and bubbling. Serve immediately.

Baked Tortellini with Three Cheeses

Serve this straight out of the oven while the cheese is still runny. If smoked mozzarella cheese is not available, try using a smoked German cheese or even grated smoked Cheddar.

Serves 4–6

INGREDIENTS
1 lb fresh tortellini
salt and pepper
2 eggs
1½ cups ricotta or cottage cheese
2 tbsp butter
1 oz fresh basil leaves
¼ lb smoked cheese, sliced
4 tbsp freshly grated Parmesan cheese

tortellini

smoked cheese

basil

eggs

1 Preheat the oven to 375°F. Cook the tortellini in plenty of boiling salted water according to the manufacturer's instructions. Drain well.

2 Beat the eggs with the ricotta cheese and season well with salt and pepper. Use the butter to grease an ovenproof dish. Spoon in half the tortellini, pour over half the ricotta mixture, and cover with half the basil leaves.

3 Cover with the smoked cheese and remaining basil. Top with the rest of the tortellini and spread over the remaining ricotta.

4 Sprinkle evenly with the Parmesan cheese. Bake in the oven for 35–45 minutes or until golden brown and bubbling. Serve immediately.

Pasta Shells with Tomatoes and Arugula

This pretty-colored pasta dish relies for its success on a salad green called arugula. Available in large supermarkets, it is a leaf easily grown in the garden or a window box and tastes slightly peppery.

Serves 4

INGREDIENTS
1 lb shell pasta
salt and pepper
1 lb very ripe cherry tomatoes
3 tbsp olive oil
3 oz fresh arugula
Parmesan cheese

olive oil

pasta shells

cherry tomatoes

arugula

Parmesan cheese

1 Cook the pasta in plenty of boiling salted water according to the manufacturer's instructions. Drain well.

2 Halve the tomatoes. Trim, wash, and dry the arugula.

3 Heat the oil in a large saucepan, add the tomatoes, and cook for barely 1 minute. The tomatoes should only just heat through and not disintegrate.

4 Shave the Parmesan cheese using a rotary vegetable peeler.

5 Add the pasta, then the arugula. Carefully stir to mix and heat through. Season well with salt and freshly ground black pepper. Serve immediately with plenty of shaved Parmesan cheese.

Pasta Tossed with Broiled Vegetables

A hearty dish to be eaten with crusty bread and washed down with a robust red wine. Try barbecuing the vegetables for a really smoky flavor.

Serves 4

INGREDIENTS
1 medium eggplant
2 medium zucchini
1 medium red bell pepper
8 garlic cloves, unpeeled
about ⅔ cup good olive oil
salt and pepper
1 lb ribbon pasta (pappardelle)
few sprigs fresh thyme, to garnish

1 Preheat the broiler. Slice the eggplant and zucchini lengthwise.

2 Halve the bell pepper, cut out the stalk and white pith, and scrape out the seeds. Slice lengthwise into 8 pieces.

3 Line a broiler pan with foil and arrange the vegetables and unpeeled garlic in a single layer on top. Brush liberally with oil and season well with salt and pepper.

olive oil

zucchini

eggplant

ribbon pasta

thyme

garlic

pepper

4 Grill until slightly charred, turning once. If necessary, cook the vegetables in 2 batches.

5 Cool the garlic, remove the charred skins, and halve. Toss the vegetables with olive oil and keep warm.

6 Meanwhile, cook the pasta in plenty of boiling salted water according to the manufacturer's instructions. Drain well and toss with the grilled vegetables. Serve immediately, garnished with sprigs of thyme and accompanied by plenty of country bread.

Green Pasta with Avocado Sauce

This is an unusual sauce with a pale green color, studded with red tomato. It has a luxurious velvety texture. The sauce is rich, so you don't need much for a filling meal.

Serves 6

INGREDIENTS
3 ripe tomatoes
2 large ripe avocados
2 tbsp butter, plus extra for tossing
    the pasta
1 garlic clove, crushed
1½ cups heavy cream
salt and pepper
dash of Tabasco sauce
1 lb green tagliatelle
freshly grated Parmesan cheese
4 tbsp sour cream

tagliatelle

tomatoes

avocado

garlic

1 Halve the tomatoes and remove the cores. Squeeze out the seeds and cut the tomatoes into dice. Set aside.

2 Halve the avocados, take out the pits, and peel. Roughly chop the flesh.

3 Melt the butter in a saucepan and add the garlic. Cook for 1 minute, then add the cream and chopped avocados. Raise the heat, stirring constantly to break up the avocados.

4 Add the diced tomatoes and season to taste with salt, pepper, and a little Tabasco sauce. Keep warm.

5 Cook the pasta in plenty of boiling salted water according to the manufacturer's instructions. Drain well and toss with a knob of butter.

6 Divide the pasta between 4 warmed bowls and spoon over the sauce. Sprinkle with grated Parmesan and top with a spoonful of sour cream.

Spaghetti with Creamy Mussel and Saffron Sauce

In this recipe the pasta is tossed with a delicious pale yellow mussel sauce, streaked with yellow threads of saffron. Powdered saffron will do just as well, but don't use turmeric – the flavor will be too strong.

Serves 4

INGREDIENTS
2 lb live mussels
⅔ cup dry white wine
2 shallots, finely chopped
2 tbsp butter
2 garlic cloves, crushed
2 tsp cornstarch
1¼ cups heavy cream
pinch of saffron threads
salt and pepper
juice of ½ lemon
1 egg yolk
1 lb spaghetti
chopped fresh parsley, to garnish

1 Scrub the mussels and rinse well. Pull off any 'beards' and leave the shellfish to soak in cold water for 30 minutes. Tap each mussel sharply after this time. Any that do not close immediately are dead and should be thrown away.

2 Drain the mussels and place in a large saucepan. Add the wine and shallots, cover, and cook (shaking frequently) over a high heat for 5–10 minutes until the mussels are open. If some do not open at this stage, throw them out.

3 Pass through a strainer, reserving the liquid. Remove most of the mussels from their shells. Reserve some in the shell to use as a garnish. Boil the reserved liquid rapidly in a medium saucepan until reduced by half.

spaghetti   *parsley*

mussels

garlic   *shallots*

4 Melt the butter in another saucepan, add the garlic, and cook until golden. Stir in the cornstarch and gradually stir in the cooking liquid and the cream. Add the saffron and seasoning and simmer until slightly thickened.

5 Stir in lemon juice to taste, then the egg yolk and mussels. Keep warm, but do not boil.

6 Cook the pasta in plenty of boiling salted water according to the manufacturer's instructions. Drain well. Toss the mussels with the spaghetti, garnish with the reserved mussels in their shells, and sprinkle with the chopped parsley. Serve immediately with lots of crusty bread.

Pasta Spirals with Pepperoni and Tomato Sauce

A warming supper dish, perfect for cold winter nights. All types of sausage are suitable, but if using raw sausages, make sure that they go in with the onion to cook thoroughly.

Serves 4

INGREDIENTS
1 medium onion
1 red bell pepper
1 green bell pepper
2 tbsp olive oil, plus extra for tossing the pasta
1¾ lb canned chopped tomatoes
2 tbsp tomato paste
2 tsp paprika
6 oz pepperoni or chorizo (spicy sausage)
3 tbsp chopped fresh parsley
salt and pepper
1 lb pasta spirals (fusilli)

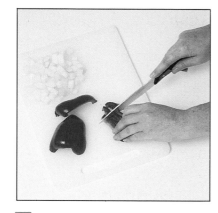

1 Chop the onion. Halve and seed the bell peppers, removing the cores, then cut the flesh into dice.

pasta spirals

pepperoni

bell peppers

onion

parsley

2 Heat the oil in a medium saucepan, add the onion, and cook for 2–3 minutes until beginning to color. Stir in the bell peppers, tomatoes, tomato paste, and paprika, bring to a boil and simmer, uncovered, for 15–20 minutes until reduced and thickened.

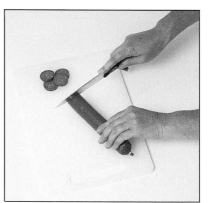

3 Slice the pepperoni and stir into the sauce with 2 tbsp chopped parsley. Season to taste.

4 While the sauce is simmering, cook the pasta in plenty of boiling salted water according to the manufacturer's instructions. Drain well. Toss the pasta with the remaining parsley and a little extra olive oil. Divide between warmed bowls and top with the sauce.

Spaghetti with Tomato and Clam Sauce

Small sweet clams make this a delicately succulent sauce. Mussels would make a good substitute, but don't be tempted to use seafood pickled in vinegar – the result will be inedible!

Serves 4

INGREDIENTS

2 lb live small clams, or 2 × 14 oz cans clams in brine, drained
6 tbsp olive oil
2 garlic cloves, crushed
1 lb 5 oz canned chopped tomatoes
3 tbsp chopped fresh parsley
salt and pepper
1 lb spaghetti

spaghetti

olive oil

parsley

garlic

clams

1 If using live clams, place them in a bowl of cold water and rinse several times to remove any grit or sand. Drain.

2 Heat the oil in a saucepan and add the clams. Stir over a high heat until the clams open. Throw away any that do not open. Transfer the clams to a bowl with a perforated spoon.

3 Reduce the clam juice left in the pan to almost nothing by boiling fast; this will also concentrate the flavor. Add the garlic and fry until golden. Pour in the tomatoes, bring to a boil, and cook for 3–4 minutes until reduced. Stir in the clam mixture or canned clams, and half the parsley and heat through. Season.

4 Cook the pasta in plenty of boiling salted water according to the manufacturer's instructions. Drain well and transfer to a warm serving dish. Pour over the sauce and sprinkle with the remaining parsley.

Pasta with Tuna, Capers, and Anchovies

This piquant sauce could be made without the addition of tomatoes – just heat the oil, add the other ingredients, and heat through gently before tossing with the pasta.

Serves 4

INGREDIENTS
14 oz canned tuna fish in oil
2 tbsp olive oil
2 garlic cloves, crushed
1¾ lb canned chopped tomatoes
6 canned anchovy fillets, drained
2 tbsp capers in vinegar, drained
2 tbsp chopped fresh basil
salt and pepper
1 lb rigatoni, garganelle or penne
fresh basil sprigs, to garnish

1 Drain the oil from the tuna into a saucepan, add the olive oil, and heat gently until it stops 'spitting'.

2 Add the garlic and fry until golden. Stir in the tomatoes and simmer for 25 minutes until thickened.

3 Flake the tuna and cut the anchovies in half. Stir into the sauce with the capers and chopped basil. Season well.

olive oil

rigatoni

tuna fish

basil

anchovy fillets

capers

garlic

4 Cook the pasta in plenty of boiling salted water according to the manufacturer's instructions. Drain well and toss with the sauce. Garnish with fresh basil sprigs.

Pasta Bows with Smoked Salmon and Dill

In Italy, pasta cooked with smoked salmon is becoming very fashionable. This is a quick and luxurious sauce.

Serves 4

INGREDIENTS
6 scallions, sliced
4 tbsp butter
6 tbsp dry white wine or vermouth
2 cups heavy cream
salt and pepper
freshly grated nutmeg
½ lb smoked salmon
2 tbsp chopped fresh dill or 1 tbsp
  dried dill
freshly squeezed lemon juice
1 lb pasta bows (farfalle)

pasta bows

lemon

scallions

smoked salmon

nutmeg

dill

1 Slice the scallions finely. Melt the butter in a saucepan and fry the scallions for 1 minute until softened.

2 Add the wine and boil hard to reduce to about 2 tbsp. Stir in the cream and add salt, pepper, and nutmeg to taste. Bring to a boil and simmer for 2–3 minutes until slightly thickened.

3 Cut the smoked salmon into 1 in squares and stir into the sauce with the dill. Taste and add a little lemon juice. Keep warm.

4 Cook the pasta in plenty of boiling salted water according to the manufacturer's instructions. Drain well. Toss the pasta with the sauce and serve immediately.

Shrimp with Tagliatelle and Pesto in Packets

A quick and impressive dish that is easy to prepare in advance and cook at the last minute. When the packets are opened, the filling smells wonderful.

Serves 4

INGREDIENTS

1½ lb medium raw shrimp, shells on
1 lb tagliatelle or similar pasta
salt and pepper
⅔ cup fresh pesto sauce or ready-made equivalent
4 tsp olive oil
1 garlic clove, crushed
8 tbsp dry white wine

tagliatelle

olive oil

pesto sauce

shrimp

garlic

1 Preheat the oven to 400°F. Twist the heads off the shrimp and discard.

2 Cook the tagliatelle in plenty of boiling salted water for 2 minutes only, then drain. Mix with half the pesto.

3 Cut 4 × 12 in squares of parchment paper and place 1 tsp olive oil in the center of each. Pile equal amounts of pasta in the middle of each square.

4 Top with equal amounts of shrimp and spoon the remaining pesto mixed with the crushed garlic over the shrimp. Season with black pepper and sprinkle each serving with 2 tbsp wine.

5 Brush the edges of the paper lightly with water and bring them loosely up around the filling, twisting tightly to enclose. (The parcels should look like money bags!)

6 Place the parcels on a baking sheet. Bake in the oven for 10–15 minutes. Serve immediately, allowing each person to open their own packet.

Rigatoni with Spicy Sausage and Tomato Sauce

This is really a shortcut to Bolognese sauce, using the wonderful fresh spicy sausages sold at every Italian grocers.

Serves 4

INGREDIENTS
1 lb fresh spicy Italian sausage
2 tbsp olive oil
1 medium onion, chopped
2 cups tomato coulis (strained, crushed tomatoes)
⅔ cup dry red wine
6 sun-dried tomatoes in oil, drained
salt and pepper
1 lb rigatoni or similar pasta
freshly grated Parmesan cheese, to serve

rigatoni

Italian sausage

Parmesan cheese

onion

sun-dried tomatoes

1 Squeeze the sausages out of their skins into a bowl and break up the meat.

2 Heat the oil in a medium saucepan and add the onion. Cook for 5 minutes until soft and golden. Stir in the sausage meat, browning it all over and breaking up the lumps with a wooden spoon. Pour in the coulis and the wine. Bring to a boil.

3 Slice the sun-dried tomatoes and add to the sauce. Simmer for 3 minutes until reduced, stirring occasionally. Season to taste.

4 Cook the pasta in plenty of boiling salted water according to the manufacturer's instructions. Drain well and top with the sauce. Serve with grated Parmesan cheese.

Pasta with Fresh Tomato and Smoky Bacon Sauce

A wonderful sauce to prepare in mid-summer when the tomatoes are ripe and sweet.

Serves 4

INGREDIENTS
2 lb ripe tomatoes
6 slices bacon
4 tbsp butter
1 medium onion, chopped
salt and pepper
1 tbsp chopped fresh oregano or 1 tsp
   dried oregano
1 lb pasta, any variety
freshly grated Parmesan cheese, to
   serve

pasta

oregano

tomatoes

onion

bacon

Parmesan cheese

1 Plunge the tomatoes into boiling water for 1 minute, then into cold water to stop them from becoming mushy. Slip off the skins. Halve the tomatoes, remove the seeds and cores, and roughly chop the flesh.

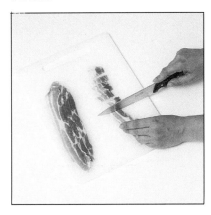

2 Remove the rind and roughly chop the bacon.

3 Melt the butter in a saucepan and add the bacon. Fry until lightly brown, then add the onion and cook gently for 5 minutes until softened. Add the tomatoes, salt, pepper, and oregano. Simmer gently for 10 minutes.

4 Cook the pasta in plenty of boiling salted water according to the manufacturer's instructions. Drain well and toss with the sauce. Serve with grated Parmesan cheese.

Pasta with Shrimp and Feta Cheese

This dish combines the richness of fresh shrimp with the tartness of feta cheese. Goat cheese could be used as an alternative.

Serves 4

INGREDIENTS
1 lb medium raw shrimp
6 scallions
4 tbsp butter
½ lb feta cheese
salt and pepper
small bunch fresh chives
1 lb penne, garganelle, or rigatoni

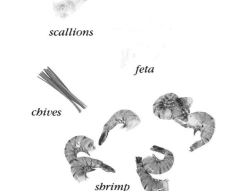

penne

scallions

feta

chives

shrimp

1 Remove the heads from the shrimp by twisting and pulling off. Peel the shrimp and discard the shells. Chop the scallions.

2 Melt the butter in a skillet and stir in the shrimp. When they turn pink, add the scallions and cook gently for 1 minute.

3 Cut the feta into ½ in cubes.

4 Stir the feta cheese into the shrimp mixture, and season with plenty of black pepper.

5 Cut the chives into 1 in lengths and stir half into the shrimp.

6 Cook the pasta in plenty of boiling salted water according to the manufacturer's instructions. Drain well, pile into a warmed serving dish, and top with the sauce. Scatter with the remaining chives and serve.

Tagliatelle with Prosciutto and Parmesan

A really simple dish, prepared in minutes from the best ingredients.

Serves 4

INGREDIENTS
¼ lb prosciutto
1 lb tagliatelle
salt and pepper
6 tbsp butter
½ cup freshly grated Parmesan
   cheese
few fresh sage leaves, to garnish

tagliatelle

sage

prosciutto

Parmesan cheese

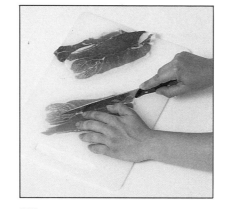

1 Cut the prosciutto into strips the same width as the tagliatelle. Cook the pasta in plenty of boiling salted water according to manufacturer's instructions.

2 Meanwhile, melt the butter gently in a saucepan, stir in the prosciutto strips and heat through, but do not fry.

3 Drain the tagliatelle well and pile into a warm serving dish.

4 Sprinkle over all the Parmesan cheese and pour over the buttery prosciutto. Season well with black pepper and garnish with the sage leaves.

Pasta with Spinach and Anchovy Sauce

Deliciously earthy, this would make a good entree or light supper dish. Add golden raisins for something really special.

Serves 4

INGREDIENTS

2 lb fresh spinach or 1 ¼ lb frozen leaf
  spinach, thawed
1 lb angel hair pasta
salt
4 tbsp olive oil
3 tbsp pine nuts
2 garlic cloves, crushed
6 canned anchovy fillets or whole
  salted anchovies, drained and
  chopped
butter, for tossing the pasta

olive oil

pine nuts

spinach

anchovy fillets

garlic   *angel hair pasta*

1 Wash the spinach well and remove the tough stalks. Drain thoroughly. Place in a large saucepan with only the water that still clings to the leaves. Cover with a lid and cook over a high heat, shaking the pan occasionally, until the spinach is just wilted and still bright green. Drain.

2 Cook the pasta in plenty of boiling salted water according to the manufacturer's instructions.

3 Heat the oil in a saucepan and fry the pine nuts until golden. Remove with a perforated spoon. Add the garlic to the oil in the pan and fry until golden. Add the anchovies.

4 Stir in the spinach, and cook for 2–3 minutes or until heated through. Stir in the pine nuts. Drain the pasta, toss in a little butter, and transfer to a warmed serving bowl. Top with the sauce and fork through roughly.

Lasagne al Forno

The classic version of this dish is pasta layered with meat sauce and creamy béchamel sauce. You could vary it by using mozzarella cheese instead of the béchamel sauce, or by mixing ricotta cheese, Parmesan, and herbs together instead of the traditional meat sauce.

Serves 4–6

INGREDIENTS
about 12 sheets dried lasagne
1 recipe Bolognese Sauce
about ½ cup freshly grated Parmesan
    cheese
tomato slices and parsley sprig, to
    garnish

BÉCHAMEL SAUCE
3¾ cups milk
sliced onion, carrot, celery
few whole peppercorns
½ cup butter
⅔ cup all-purpose flour
salt and pepper
freshly grated nutmeg

1 First make the béchamel sauce. Pour the milk into a saucepan and add the vegetables and peppercorns. Bring to boiling point, remove from the heat, and leave to infuse for at least 30 minutes.

2 Strain the milk into a pitcher. Melt the butter in the same saucepan and stir in the flour. Cook, stirring, for 2 minutes.

3 Remove from the heat and add the milk all at once, whisk well, and return to the heat. Bring to a boil, whisking all the time, then simmer for 2–3 minutes, stirring constantly until thickened. Season to taste with salt, pepper, and nutmeg.

lasagne

carrot

onion

celery

Parmesan cheese   *Bolognese Sauce*

4 Preheat the oven to 350°F. If necessary, cook the sheets of lasagne in plenty of boiling salted water according to the instructions. Lift out with a perforated spoon and drain on a clean dish towel. Spoon one-third of the meat sauce into a buttered baking dish.

5 Cover the meat sauce with 4 sheets of lasagne and spread with one-third of the béchamel sauce. Repeat twice more, finishing with a layer of béchamel sauce covering the whole top.

6 Sprinkle with Parmesan cheese and bake in the oven for about 45 minutes until brown. Serve garnished with tomato slices and a sprig of parsley.

Cannelloni al Forno

A lighter alternative to the usual beef-filled, béchamel-coated version. Fill with ricotta, onion, and mushroom for a vegetarian recipe.

Serves 4–6

INGREDIENTS
4 cups boneless, skinned chicken
   breast, cooked
½ lb mushrooms
2 garlic cloves, crushed
2 tbsp chopped fresh parsley
1 tbsp chopped fresh tarragon
1 egg, beaten
salt and pepper
fresh lemon juice
12–18 cannelloni tubes
1 recipe Napoletana Sauce
½ cup freshly grated Parmesan
   cheese
1 sprig fresh parsley, to garnish

1 Preheat the oven to 400°F. Place the chicken in a food processor and blend until finely ground. Transfer to a bowl.

2 Place the mushrooms, garlic, parsley, and tarragon in the food processor and blend until finely minced.

3 Beat the mushroom mixture into the chicken with the egg, salt and pepper, and lemon juice to taste.

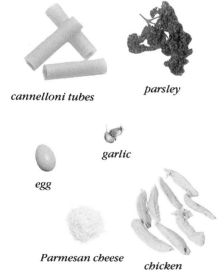

cannelloni tubes   *parsley*

egg   *garlic*

Parmesan cheese   *chicken*

4 If necessary, cook the cannelloni in plenty of salted boiling water according to the manufacturer's instructions. Drain well on a clean dish towel.

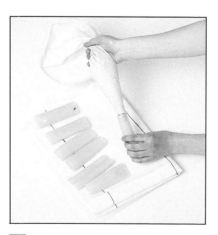

5 Place the filling in a pastry bag fitted with a large plain tip. Use this to fill each tube of cannelloni.

6 Lay the filled cannelloni tightly together in a single layer in a buttered shallow ovenproof dish. Spoon over the tomato sauce and sprinkle with Parmesan cheese. Bake in the oven for 30 minutes, or until brown and bubbling. Serve garnished with a sprig of parsley.

Spaghetti alla Carbonara

It has been said that this dish was originally cooked by Italian coal miners, or charcoal-burners, hence the name 'carbonara'. The secret of its creamy sauce is not to overcook the egg.

Serves 4

INGREDIENTS
6 oz bacon
1 garlic clove, chopped
3 eggs
1 lb spaghetti
salt and pepper
4 tbsp freshly grated Parmesan cheese

bacon

garlic

eggs　　*spaghetti*

Parmesan cheese

1 Cut the bacon into a dice and place in a medium saucepan. Place over the heat and fry in its own fat with the garlic until brown. Keep warm until needed.

2 Whisk the eggs together in a bowl.

3 Cook the spaghetti in plenty of boiling salted water according to the manufacturer's instructions until *al dente*. Drain well.

4 Quickly transfer the spaghetti to the pan with the bacon and stir in the eggs, a little salt, lots of pepper, and half the cheese. Toss well to mix. The eggs should half-cook with the heat from the spaghetti. Serve in warm bowls with the remaining cheese.

Pasta with Bolognese Sauce

Traditional Bolognese sauce contains chicken livers to add richness, but you can leave them out and replace with an equal quantity of ground beef.

Serves 4–6

INGREDIENTS
3 oz pancetta or bacon in a piece
4 oz chicken livers
4 tbsp butter, plus extra for tossing
  the pasta
1 medium onion, finely chopped
1 medium carrot, diced
1 celery stick, finely chopped
½ lb lean ground beef
2 tbsp tomato paste
½ cup dry white wine
1 cup beef stock or water
salt and pepper
freshly grated nutmeg
1 lb tagliatelle, spaghetti, or fettuccine
freshly grated Parmesan cheese, to
  serve

COOK'S TIP
If you like a richer sauce, stir in ⅔ cup heavy cream or milk when the sauce has finished cooking.

1 Cut the pancetta into a dice. Trim the chicken livers, removing any fat or gristle and any 'green' bits, which will be bitter if left on. Roughly chop the livers.

2 Melt 4 tbsp butter in a saucepan and add the bacon. Cook for 2–3 minutes until beginning to brown. Add the onion, carrot, and celery and brown these too.

3 Stir in the ground beef and brown over a high heat, breaking it up with a spoon. Stir in the chicken livers and cook for 2–3 minutes. Add the tomato paste, mix well, and pour in the wine and stock. Season well with salt, pepper, and nutmeg. Bring to a boil, cover, and simmer gently for about 35 minutes, stirring occasionally.

4 Cook the pasta in plenty of boiling salted water according to the manufacturer's instructions. Drain well and toss with the extra butter. Toss the meat sauce with the pasta and serve with plenty of Parmesan cheese.

tagliatelle

carrot

chicken livers

onion

celery

bacon

ground beef

Fettuccine all'Alfredo

A classic dish from Rome, Fettuccine all'Alfredo is simply pasta tossed with heavy cream, butter, and freshly grated Parmesan cheese. Popular less classic additions are peas and strips of ham.

Serves 4

INGREDIENTS
2 tbsp butter
²⁄₃ cup heavy cream, plus 4 tbsp extra
1 lb fettuccine
freshly grated nutmeg
½ cup freshly grated Parmesan
   cheese, plus extra to serve
salt and pepper

fettuccine

nutmeg

Parmesan cheese

1 Place the butter and ²⁄₃ cup cream in a heavy saucepan, bring to a boil, and simmer for 1 minute until slightly thickened.

2 Cook the fettuccine in plenty of boiling salted water according to the manufacturer's instructions, but for 2 minutes less time. The pasta should still be a little firm.

3 Drain very well and transfer to the pan with the cream sauce.

4 Place on the heat and toss the pasta in the sauce to coat.

5 Add the extra 4 tbsp cream, the cheese, salt and pepper to taste, and a little grated nutmeg. Toss until well coated and heated through. Serve immediately with extra grated Parmesan cheese.

Spaghetti Olio e Aglio

This is another classic recipe from Rome. A quick and filling dish, originally the food of the poor involving nothing more than pasta, garlic, and olive oil, but now fast becoming fashionable.

Serves 4

INGREDIENTS
2 garlic cloves
2 tbsp fresh parsley
½ cup olive oil
1 lb spaghetti
salt and pepper

spaghetti

olive oil

parsley

garlic

1 Finely chop the garlic.

2 Chop the parsley roughly.

3 Heat the olive oil in a medium saucepan and add the garlic and a pinch of salt. Cook gently, stirring all the time, until golden. If the garlic becomes too brown, it will taste bitter.

4 Meanwhile cook the spaghetti in plenty of boiling salted water according to the manufacturer's instructions. Drain well.

5 Toss with the warm – not sizzling – garlic and oil and add plenty of black pepper and the parsley. Serve immediately.

Paglia e Fieno

The title of this dish translates as 'straw and hay', which refers to the yellow and green colors of the pasta when mixed together. Using fresh peas makes all the difference to this dish.

Serves 4

INGREDIENTS
4 tbsp butter
2 cups frozen petits pois (small peas) or 2 lb fresh peas, shelled
⅔ cup heavy cream, plus 4 tbsp extra
1 lb tagliatelle (plain and spinach, mixed)
½ cup freshly grated Parmesan cheese, plus extra to serve
salt and pepper
freshly grated nutmeg

tagliatelle

peas

Parmesan cheese

COOK'S TIP
Sautéed mushrooms and narrow strips of cooked ham also make a good addition.

1 Melt the butter in a heavy saucepan and add the peas. Sauté for 2–3 minutes, then add the cream, bring to a boil, and simmer for 1 minute until slightly thickened.

2 Cook the fettuccine in plenty of boiling salted water according to the manufacturer's instructions, but for 2 minutes' less time. The pasta should still be *al dente*. Drain very well and transfer to the pan with the cream and pea sauce.

3 Place on the heat and toss the pasta in the sauce to coat. Pour in the extra cream, the cheese, salt and pepper to taste, and a little grated nutmeg. Toss until well coated and heated through. Serve immediately with extra Parmesan cheese.

Pasta Napoletana

The simple classic cooked tomato sauce with no adornments!

Serves 4

INGREDIENTS

2 lb fresh ripe red tomatoes or 1¾ lb
  canned plum tomatoes with juice
1 medium onion, chopped
1 medium carrot, diced
1 celery stick, diced
⅔ cup dry white wine (optional)
1 sprig fresh parsley
salt and pepper
pinch of superfine sugar
1 tbsp chopped fresh oregano or 1 tsp
  dried oregano
1 lb pasta, any variety
freshly grated Parmesan cheese, to
  serve

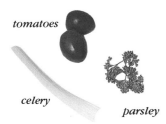

pasta

onion

tomatoes

celery

parsley

carrot

Parmesan cheese

1 Roughly chop the tomatoes and place in a medium saucepan.

2 Put all the ingredients – except the oregano, pasta, and cheese – into the pan with the tomatoes. Bring to a boil and simmer, half-covered, for 45 minutes until very thick, stirring occasionally. Pass through a strainer or liquidize and strain to remove the tomato seeds, then stir in the oregano. Taste to check the seasoning and adjust if necessary.

3 Cook the pasta in plenty of boiling salted water according to the manufacturer's instructions. Drain well.

4 Toss the pasta with the sauce. Serve with grated Parmesan cheese.

Pasta with Pesto Sauce

Don't skimp on the fresh basil – this is the most wonderful sauce in the world! This pesto can also be used as a basting sauce for broiled chicken or fish, or rubbed over a leg of lamb before baking.

Serves 4

INGREDIENTS
2 garlic cloves
salt and pepper
½ cup pine nuts
1 cup fresh basil leaves
⅔ cup olive oil (not extra-virgin as it is too strong)
4 tbsp unsalted butter, softened
4 tbsp freshly grated Parmesan cheese
1 lb spaghetti

olive oil

spaghetti

pine nuts

Parmesan cheese

basil

1 Peel the garlic and process in a food processor with a little salt and the pine nuts until broken up. Add the basil leaves and continue mixing to a paste.

2 Gradually add the olive oil, little by little, until the mixture is creamy and thick.

3 Mix in the butter and season with pepper. Mix in the cheese. (Alternatively, you can make the pesto by hand using a pestle and mortar.)

4 Store the pesto in a jar (with a layer of olive oil on top to exclude the air) in the fridge until needed.

5 Cook the pasta in plenty of boiling salted water according to the manufacturer's instructions. Drain well.

COOK'S TIP

A good pesto can be made using parsley instead of basil and walnuts instead of pine nuts. To make it go further, add a spoonful or two of fromage frais. 'Red' pesto includes sun-dried tomato paste and pounded roasted red peppers.

6 Toss the pasta with half the pesto and serve in warm bowls with the remaining pesto spooned on top.

Rotolo di Pasta

A giant jelly roll of pasta with a spinach filling, that is poached, sliced, and baked with béchamel or tomato sauce. Use fresh homemade pasta for this recipe, or ask your local Italian grocer to make a large sheet of pasta for you.

Serves 6

INGREDIENTS

1 ½ lb frozen chopped spinach, thawed
4 tbsp butter
1 medium onion, chopped
4 oz ham or bacon, diced
½ lb ricotta or cottage cheese
1 egg
salt and pepper
freshly grated nutmeg
fresh spinach pasta made with 2 eggs and 1¾ cups flour
5½ cups Béchamel Sauce, warmed
½ cup freshly grated Parmesan cheese

onion

ricotta cheese

spinach

nutmeg

ham

1 Squeeze the excess moisture from the spinach and set aside.

2 Melt the butter in a saucepan and fry the onion until golden. Add the ham and fry until beginning to brown. Take off the heat and stir in the spinach. Cool slightly, then beat in the ricotta and egg. Season well with salt, pepper, and nutmeg.

3 Roll the pasta out to a rectangle about 12 × 16 in. Spread the filling all over, leaving a ½ in border all around the edge.

4 Roll up from the shorter end and wrap in cheesecloth to form a 'sausage', tying the ends securely with string. Poach in a very large pan (or fish poacher) of simmering water for 20 minutes or until firm. Carefully remove, drain, and unwrap. Cool.

5 When you are ready to finish the dish, preheat the oven to 400°F. Cut the pasta roll into 1 in slices. Spoon a little béchamel sauce over the base of a shallow baking dish and arrange the slices slightly overlapping each other.

6 Spoon over the remaining sauce, sprinkle with the cheese, and bake in the oven for 15–20 minutes or until browned and bubbling. Allow to stand for a few minutes before serving.

Pasta, Melon and Shrimp Salad

Orange-fleshed cantaloupe or Charentais melon looks spectacular in this salad. You could also use a mixture of honeydew, cantaloupe and watermelon.

Serves 4–6

INGREDIENTS
1½ cups pasta shapes
½ lb frozen shrimp, thawed and
    drained
1 large or 2 small melons
4 tbsp olive oil
1 tbsp tarragon vinegar
2 tbsp chopped fresh chives or parsley
sprigs of herbs, to garnish
Napa cabbage, to serve

melons

pasta shapes

shrimp

Napa cabbage

1 Cook the pasta in boiling salted water according to the manufacturer's instructions. Drain well and allow to cool.

2 Peel the shrimp and discard the shells.

3 Halve the melon and remove the seeds with a teaspoon. Carefully scoop the flesh into balls with a melon baller and mix with the shrimp and pasta.

4 Whisk the oil, vinegar, and chopped herbs together. Pour on to the shrimp mixture and toss to coat. Cover and chill for at least 30 minutes.

5 Meanwhile shred the Napa cabbage and use to line a shallow bowl or the empty melon halves.

6 Pile the shrimp mixture onto the Napa cabbage and garnish with herbs.

Avocado, Tomato, and Mozzarella Pasta Salad with Pine Nuts

A salad made from ingredients representing the colors of the Italian flag — a sunny cheerful dish!

Serves 4

INGREDIENTS
1½ cups pasta bows (farfalle)
6 ripe red tomatoes
½ lb mozzarella cheese
1 large ripe avocado
2 tbsp pine nuts, toasted
1 sprig fresh basil, to garnish

DRESSING
6 tbsp olive oil
2 tbsp wine vinegar
1 tsp balsamic vinegar (optional)
1 tsp whole-grain mustard
pinch of sugar
salt and pepper
2 tbsp chopped fresh basil

olive oil

avocado

tomatoes

basil

mozzarella cheese

pine nuts   *pasta bows*

1 Cook the pasta in plenty of boiling salted water according to the manufacturer's instructions. Drain well and cool.

2 Slice the tomatoes and mozzarella cheese into thin rounds.

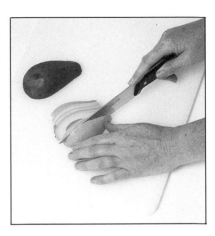

3 Halve the avocado, remove the pit, and peel off the skin. Slice the flesh lengthwise.

4 Whisk all the dressing ingredients together in a small bowl.

5 Arrange the tomato, mozzarella, and avocado in overlapping slices around the edge of a flat plate.

6 Toss the pasta with half the dressing and the chopped basil. Pile into the center of the plate. Pour over the remaining dressing, scatter over the pine nuts, and garnish with a sprig of fresh basil. Serve immediately.

Whole-wheat Pasta, Asparagus, and Potato Salad with Parmesan

A meal in itself, this is a real treat when made with fresh asparagus just in season.

Serves 4

INGREDIENTS
½ lb whole-wheat pasta shapes
4 tbsp extra-virgin olive oil
salt and pepper
12 oz baby new potatoes
½ lb fresh asparagus
¼ lb piece fresh Parmesan cheese

olive oil

asparagus

Parmesan cheese

pasta shapes

new potatoes

1 Cook the pasta in boiling salted water according to the manufacturer's instructions. Drain well and toss with the olive oil, salt, and pepper while still warm.

2 Wash the potatoes and cook in boiling salted water for 12–15 minutes or until tender. Drain and toss with the pasta.

3 Trim any woody ends off the asparagus and halve the stalks if very long. Blanch in boiling salted water for 6 minutes until bright green and still crunchy. Drain. Plunge into cold water to stop them cooking and allow to cool. Drain and dry on paper towels.

4 Toss the asparagus with the potatoes and pasta, season, and transfer to a shallow bowl. Using a rotary vegetable peeler, shave the Parmesan cheese over the salad.

Roquefort and Walnut Pasta Salad

This is a simple earthy salad, relying totally on the quality of the ingredients. There is no real substitute for the Roquefort — a blue-veined ewe's-milk cheese from southwestern France.

Serves 4

INGREDIENTS
½ lb pasta shapes
selection of salad leaves (such as arugula, frisée, lamb's lettuce, baby spinach, radicchio, etc.)
2 tbsp walnut oil
4 tbsp sunflower oil
2 tbsp red-wine vinegar or sherry vinegar
salt and pepper
½ lb Roquefort cheese, roughly crumbled
1 cup walnut halves

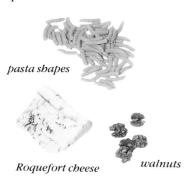

pasta shapes

Roquefort cheese   *walnuts*

salad leaves

COOK'S TIP
Try toasting the walnuts under the broiler for a couple of minutes to release the flavor.

1 Cook the pasta in plenty of boiling salted water according to the manufacturer's instructions. Drain well and cool. Wash and dry the salad leaves and place in a bowl.

2 Whisk together the walnut oil, sunflower oil, vinegar, and salt and pepper to taste.

3 Pile the pasta in the center of the leaves, scatter over the crumbled Roquefort, and pour over the dressing.

4 Scatter over the walnuts. Toss just before serving.

Mediterranean Salad with Basil

A type of Salade Niçoise with pasta, conjuring up all the sunny flavors of the Mediterranean.

Serves 4

INGREDIENTS
½ lb chunky pasta shapes
6 oz fine green beans
2 large ripe tomatoes
2 oz fresh basil leaves
7 oz can tuna fish in oil, drained
2 hard-cooked eggs, shelled and sliced
    or quartered
2 oz can anchovies, drained
capers and black olives

DRESSING
6 tbsp extra-virgin olive oil
2 tbsp white-wine vinegar or lemon
    juice
2 garlic cloves, crushed
½ tsp Dijon mustard
2 tbsp chopped fresh basil
salt and pepper

tomatoes

olive oil

garlic

basil

pasta

egg

anchovies

green beans

tuna fish

1 Whisk all the ingredients for the dressing together and leave to infuse while you make the salad.

2 Cook the pasta in plenty of boiling salted water according to the manufacturer's instructions. Drain well and cool.

3 Trim the beans and blanch in boiling salted water for 3 minutes. Drain and refresh in cold water.

4 Slice or quarter the tomatoes and arrange on the bottom of a bowl. Toss with a little dressing and cover with a quarter of the basil leaves. Then cover with the beans. Toss with a little more dressing and cover with a third of the remaining basil.

5 Cover with the pasta tossed in a little more dressing, half the remaining basil and the roughly flaked tuna.

6 Arrange the eggs on top, then finally scatter over the anchovies, capers and black olives. Pour over the remaining dressing and garnish with the remaining basil. Serve immediately. Don't be tempted to chill this salad – all the flavor will be dulled.

Dark Chocolate Ravioli with White Chocolate and Cream Cheese Filling

This is a spectacular, chocolatey pasta, with cocoa powder added to the flour. The pasta packets contain a rich creamy-white filling.

Serves 4

INGREDIENTS
1 ½ cups all-purpose flour
¼ cup cocoa powder
2 tbsp confectioners' sugar
2 large eggs
salt
light cream and grated chocolate, to
    serve

FILLING
6 oz white chocolate
3 cups cream cheese
1 egg, plus 1 beaten egg to seal

eggs

cream cheese

cocoa powder

white chocolate

1 Make the pasta following the instructions for Basic Pasta Dough, but sifting the flour with the cocoa and confectioners' sugar before adding the eggs. Cover and rest for 30 minutes.

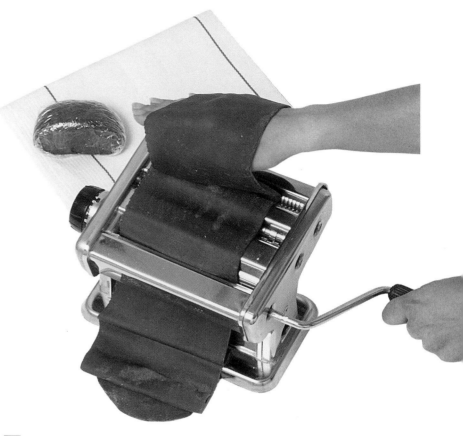

2 For the filling, break up the white chocolate and melt it in a bowl standing in a pan of barely simmering water. Cool slightly, then beat into the cream cheese with the egg. Spoon into a pastry bag fitted with a plain tip.

3 Cut the dough in half and wrap one portion in clear film (plastic wrap). Roll the pasta out thinly to a rectangle on a lightly floured surface, or use a pasta machine. Cover with a clean damp tea (dish) towel and repeat with the remaining pasta.

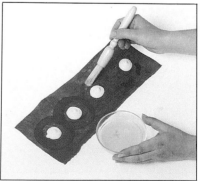

4 Pipe small mounds (about 1 tsp) of filling in even rows, spacing them at 1 ½ in intervals, across one piece of the dough. Using a pastry brush, brush the spaces of dough between the mounds with some beaten egg.

5 Using a rolling pin, lift the remaining sheet of pasta over the dough with the filling. Press down firmly between the pockets of filling, pushing out any trapped air. Cut into rounds with a serrated ravioli cutter or sharp knife. Transfer to a floured dish towel. Rest for 1 hour.

6 Bring a large pan of salted water to a boil and add the ravioli a few at a time, stirring to prevent them sticking together. Simmer gently for 3–5 minutes, remove with a perforated spoon. Serve with a generous splash of light cream and some grated chocolate.

Crisp Vermicelli Cakes with Honey and Walnuts

In this recipe the pasta is double-cooked for crispness, then soaked in honey and nuts to give a Middle Eastern flavor.

Serves 4

INGREDIENTS
½ lb vermicelli or angel hair pasta
salt
½ cup butter
1½ cups mixed nuts, such as walnuts
    and pistachios
½ cup granulated sugar
⅓ cup clear honey
2 tsp lemon juice

vermicelli

nuts

lemon

butter

honey

1 Preheat the oven to 350°F. Cook the pasta in plenty of boiling salted water according to the manufacturer's instructions. Drain well, return to the pan with the butter, and toss in the residual heat to coat. Cool.

2 Set 4 poaching rings on baking sheets. Divide the pasta into 8 mounds, then lightly press a mound of pasta evenly into each ring.

3 Chop the nuts and sprinkle half over the pasta. Top each ring with a mound of the remaining pasta and press down well. Bake in the oven for 40–45 minutes or until golden brown.

4 Meanwhile, place the sugar, honey, and ⅔ cup water in a medium saucepan and slowly bring to a boil, making sure that all the sugar is dissolved before it boils. Simmer for 10 minutes, add the lemon juice, and simmer for 5 minutes more. Set aside.

5 Carefully remove the baked pasta from the rings and place in an even layer on a shallow dish.

6 Pour over the syrup and scatter with the remaining nuts. Cool completely before serving.

Cinnamon Tagliatelle with Creamy Custard Sauce

The secret of this pudding is to roll the pasta out very thinly, giving delicious ribbons coated in a delicate vanilla sauce.

Serves 4

INGREDIENTS
1½ cups all-purpose flour
pinch of salt
2 tbsp confectioners' sugar
2 tsp ground cinnamon, plus extra for
    dusting the pasta
2 large eggs
melted butter, for tossing the pasta

CUSTARD
1 vanilla bean
2½ cups milk
6 egg yolks
¼–⅓ cup superfine sugar

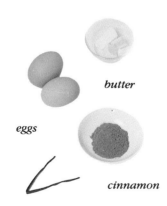

butter

eggs

cinnamon

vanilla bean

1 Make the pasta following the instructions for Basic Pasta Dough, but sifting the flour with the confectioners' sugar and cinnamon before adding the eggs. Roll out thinly and cut into tagliatelle. Spread out on a clean, lightly floured dish towel to dry.

2 For the custard, split the vanilla bean and scrape out the seeds into a saucepan. Add the pod itself to the pan with the milk and slowly bring to a boil. Take the pan off the heat and allow to infuse for 10 minutes, then strain to remove the vanilla bean and seeds.

3 Whisk the egg yolks and sugar together in a medium bowl until pale and creamy. Slowly stir in the strained milk, return the pan to a low heat, and cook, stirring, until slightly thickened. Do not boil or the custard will curdle. Strain and keep warm.

4 Drop the tagliatelle into plenty of boiling salted water and cook until the water returns to the boil or until *al dente*. The pasta should have no hard core, and should be very pliable. Strain and toss with a little butter. Serve in warm bowls with the custard poured over. Dust with extra cinnamon if liked.

Tiramisu Surprise

The small pasta shapes incorporated into this dessert make a very pretty dish served in tall glasses.

Serves 4

INGREDIENTS
¼ lb small pasta shapes
salt
16 small ratafias, macaroons, or
   Amaretti cookies
6 tbsp very strong black coffee
2 tbsp brandy
4 tbsp dark rum
1¾ cups mascarpone or other cream
   cheese
½ cup confectioners' sugar, sifted
⅔ cup whipping cream
3 oz chocolate shavings, to decorate

dark rum

pasta shapes

brandy   *chocolate*

ratafias

1 Cook the pasta in plenty of boiling salted water according to the manufacturer's instructions. Drain well and cool.

2 Place the ratafias in 4 individual glasses and spoon over a layer of pasta. Mix together the coffee, brandy, and 2 tbsp of the rum, and pour this over the pasta layer.

3 Beat the mascarpone with the sugar and remaining rum until smooth. Stir in the cream and spoon the mixture equally between the glasses.

4 Sprinkle the chocolate shavings thickly on top of the cheese mixture to decorate and refrigerate for at least 1 hour before serving.

Pasta Timbales with Apricot Sauce

Orzo, or rice-shaped, pasta inspired this dessert made like a rice pudding, but with a difference! Other small soup pastas can be used if orzo cannot be found.

Serves 4

INGREDIENTS
¼ lb orzo or other soup pasta
⅓ cup superfine sugar
salt
2 tbsp butter
1 vanilla bean, split
3⅔ cups milk
1¼ cups ready-made vanilla pudding
3 tbsp kirsch
1 tbsp powdered gelatin
oil, for greasing
14 oz canned apricots in juice
lemon juice
fresh flowers, to decorate (optional)

custard

pasta

butter

lemon

apricots

1 Place the pasta, sugar, a pinch of salt, the butter, vanilla bean, and milk into a heavy saucepan and bring to a boil. Turn down the heat and simmer for 25 minutes until the pasta is tender and most of the liquid is absorbed. Stir frequently to prevent it from sticking.

2 Remove the vanilla bean and transfer the pasta to a bowl to cool. Stir in the custard and 2 tbsp of the kirsch.

3 Sprinkle the gelatin over 3 tbsp water in a small bowl set in a pan of barely simmering water. Allow to become spongy and heat gently to dissolve. Stir into the pasta.

4 Lightly oil 4 timbale molds and spoon in the pasta. Refrigerate for about 2 hours until set.

5 Meanwhile, liquidize the apricots, pass through a strainer, and add lemon juice and kirsch to taste. Dilute with a little water if too thick.

6 Loosen the pasta timbales from their molds and turn out onto individual plates. Spoon some apricot sauce around and serve, decorated with a few fresh flowers if liked.

Strawberry Conchiglie Salad with Kirsch and Raspberry Sauce

A divinely decadent dessert laced with liqueur and luscious raspberry sauce.

Serves 4

INGREDIENTS
6 oz pasta shells (conchiglie)
salt
½ lb fresh or frozen raspberries,
    thawed if frozen
1–2 tbsp superfine sugar
lemon juice
1 lb small fresh strawberries
flaked almonds
3 tbsp kirsch

pasta shells

raspberries

strawberries

almonds

1 Cook the pasta in plenty of boiling salted water according to the manufacturer's instructions. Drain well and cool.

2 Purée the raspberries in a food processor and pass through a strainer to remove the seeds.

3 Put the purée in a small saucepan with the sugar and simmer for 5–6 minutes, stirring occasionally. Add lemon juice to taste. Set aside to cool.

4 Hull the strawberries and halve if necessary. Toss with the pasta and transfer to a serving bowl.

5 Spread the almonds on a baking sheet and toast under the broiler until golden. Cool.

6 Stir the kirsch into the raspberry sauce and pour over the salad. Scatter with the toasted almonds and serve.

INDEX

A

Anchovies: pasta with spinach and anchovy sauce, 61
  pasta with tuna, capers, and anchovies, 52
Apricots: pasta timbales with apricot sauce, 92
Asparagus: whole-wheat pasta, asparagus, and potato salad with Parmesan, 82
Avocadoes: avocado, tomato, and mozzarella pasta salad with pine nuts, 80
  green pasta with avocado sauce, 46

B

Bacon: pasta with fresh tomato and smoky bacon sauce, 57
  spaghetti alla Carbonara, 66
Basil: Mediterranean salad with basil, 84
  pesto, see Pesto
Beans: Italian bean and pasta soup, 24
Beef: pasta with Bolognese sauce, 65

C

Cannelloni al forno, 64
Capers: pasta with tuna, capers, and anchovies, 52
Cauliflower: creamy Parmesan and cauliflower soup with pasta bows, 29
Cheese, 14
  avocado, tomato, and mozzarella pasta salad with pine nuts, 80
  baked tortellini with three cheeses, 41
  creamy Parmesan and cauliflower soup with pasta bows, 29
  dark chocolate ravioli with white chocolate and cream cheese filling, 86
  fettucine all'Alfredo, 68
  tagliatelle with Gorgonzola sauce, 36
  pasta with shrimp and feta cheese, 58
  roquefort and walnut pasta salad, 83
  spaghetti alla Carbonara, 66
  tagliatelle with Prosciutto and parmesan, 60

tiramisu surprise, 91
tortellini with cream, butter, and cheese, 40
Chicken: chicken vermicelli soup with egg shreds, 28
  Thai chicken soup, 28
  cannelloni al forno, 64
Chicken livers: pasta with Bolognese sauce, 65
Chocolate: dark chocolate ravioli with white chocolate and cream cheese filling, 86
Cinnamon tagliatelle with creamy custard sauce, 90
Clams: spaghetti with tomato and clam sauce, 51
Cooking pasta, 18

E

Eastern pasta, 13
Eggs: spaghetti alla Carbonara, 66
Equipment, 16, 17

F

Fish, 14
  Provençal fish soup with pasta, 26

G

Garlic: spaghetti 'Olio e Aglio', 70

H

Herbs, 10
Honey: crisp vermicelli cakes with honey and walnuts, 88

I

Italian bean and pasta soup, 24

L

Lasagne al forno, 62

M

Macaroni, 20
Making pasta, 18–21
Mediterranean salad with basil, 84
Melon: pasta, melon, and shrimp salad, 78
Minestrone soup, 22
Mussels: spaghetti with creamy mussel and saffron sauce, 48

N

Noodles, 13
Nuts, 14

P

Paglia e Fieno, 72
Pasta dough, 18
Pasta types, 8, 9
Pastes, 12
Peas: paglia e fieno, 72
Penne with garlic crumbs, 38
Pepperoni: pasta spirals with pepperoni and tomato sauce, 50
Peppers: pasta with roasted bell pepper and tomato sauce, 30
Pesto: pasta with pesto sauce, 74
Pine nuts: avocado, tomato, and Mozzarella pasta salad with pine nuts, 80
  pesto, see Pesto
Potatoes: whole-wheat pasta, asparagus, and potato salad with Parmesan, 82
  pasta, melon, and shrimp salad, 78
Prosciutto: tagliatelle with Prosciutto and parmesan, 60
Provençal fish soup with pasta, 26

R

Raspberries: strawberry conchiglie salad with Kirsch and raspberry sauce, 95
Ravioli, 21

S

Salads: avocado, tomato, and mozzarella pasta salad with pine nuts, 80
  Mediterranean salad with basil, 84
  pasta, melon and shrimp salad, 78
  roquefort and walnut pasta salad, 83
  whole-wheat pasta, asparagus, and potato salad with Parmesan, 82
Sauces, 12
  cinnamon tagliatelle with creamy custard sauce, 90
  tagliatelle with Gorgonzola sauce, 36
  pasta Napoletana, 73

pasta spirals with pepperoni and tomato sauce, 50
  pasta timbales with apricot sauce, 92
  pasta with Bolognese sauce, 65
  pasta with fresh tomato and smoky bacon sauce, 57
  pasta with pesto sauce, 74
  pasta with roasted bell pepper and tomato sauce, 30
  pasta with spinach and anchovy sauce, 61
  pasta with tomato and cream sauce, 37
  rigatoni with spicy sausage and tomato sauce, 56
  spaghetti with creamy mussel and saffron sauce, 48
  spaghetti with fresh tomato sauce, 34
  spaghetti with tomato and clam sauce, 51
  tagliatelle with walnut sauce, 32
Sausage: rigatoni with spicy sausage and tomato sauce, 56
Shellfish, 14
Shrimp: pasta, melon, and shrimp salad, 78
  pasta with shrimp and feta cheese, 58
  pasta with tagliatelle and pesto in packets, 54
Smoked salmon: pasta bows with smoked salmon and dill, 53
Soup: chicken vermicelli soup with egg shreds, 28
  creamy Parmesan and cauliflower soup with pasta bows, 29
  Italian bean and pasta soup, 24
  minestrone, 22
  Provençal fish soup with pasta, 26
  soupe au pistou, 23
  Thai chicken soup, 28
  zucchini soup with small pasta shells, 25
Soupe au pistou, 23
Spices, 10
Spinach: pasta with spinach and anchovy sauce, 61
  rotolo di pasta, 76
Stir-fried vegetables with pasta, 33
Strawberry conchiglie salad with Kirsch and raspberry sauce, 95

T

Tagliatelle, 20
Thai chicken soup, 28
Tiramisu surprise, 91
Tomatoes: avocado, tomato, and Mozzarella pasta salad with pine nuts, 80
  pasta Napoletana, 73
  pasta spirals with pepperoni and tomato sauce, 50
  pasta with fresh tomato and smoky bacon sauce, 57
  pasta with roasted bell pepper and tomato sauce, 30
  pasta with tomato and cream sauce, 37
  rigatoni with spicy sausage and tomato sauce, 56
  spaghetti with fresh tomato sauce, 34
  spaghetti with tomato and clam sauce, 51
Tortellini, 21
Tuna: pasta with tuna, capers, and anchovies, 52

V

Vegetables, 14
  Mediterranean salad with basil, 84
  pasta tossed with grilled vegetables, 44
  stir-fried vegetables with pasta, 33

W

Walnuts: crisp vermicelli cakes with honey and walnuts, 88
  roquefort and walnut pasta salad, 83
  tagliatelle with walnut sauce, 32

Z

Zucchini soup with small pasta shells, 25